THE TEAMWORKING POCKETBOOK

By Ian Fleming

Drawings by Phil Hailstone

"Clears the fog in team dynamics and makes teamwork enjoyable as well as essential." **Steve Evans, Director of Leisure and Community Resources, South Gloucestershire Council**

"There are very few truly high-performing teams; this book provides practical tools and tips to help you ensure that the teams you belong to join the few." **Ian Anderson, Head of Lending New Business, Birmingham Midshires Building Society**

"A very reliable and practical guide for team[illegible] at all levels." **Allan J. D. Taylor, Training & Development M[illegible]ving Ltd**

CONTENTS

INTRODUCTION

This Pocketbook is for those who find themselves leading teams and for team members.

In a changing world, teams are being set up for a variety of reasons and there is a constant stream of people joining and leaving. The leader's challenge is to identify skills, build harmony and retain focus, often within tight timescales.

It is my belief - despite all that has been written - that most teams rarely perform effectively, or as planned.

There is a great deal of material available for building teams, most of which is designed to enable people to **start** to work together. Often, very little thought is given to what happens next - when they are expected to produce results, but could be experiencing problems.

This Pocketbook contains examples of common situations faced by teams and how these can be tackled.

INTRODUCTION

WHY TEAMS?

The need for teams and teamworking has never been greater, given:

- Higher customer expectations (better value for money, more choice and the need to deliver a complete package covering quality, service and support)
- More complex markets and products
- Greater commercial uncertainty (changing markets, shorter life cycles and the need to respond to demanding customers)
- Increased pressure from competition, legislation and environmental issues

All of these call for a:

- Combination of skills, experiences and judgements
- Breaking down of barriers between departments within organisations
- Closer customer relationships

Teams, as opposed to individuals, have the potential to bring together the skills, experiences and disciplines required in these changing times.

WHAT IS A TEAM?

DEFINITIONS

- 'A number of people who **co-operate** in such a way that it achieves more than the sum total of the individuals' achievements'
- 'A group of people **united by a common purpose**'
- 'An energetic group of people **committed to achieving common objectives**, who work well together and enjoy doing so, and who produce high quality results' (Improving work groups by Francis & Young)
- 'A team is a small number of people with complementary skills who are committed to a common purpose, performance goals, and approach for which they hold themselves **mutually accountable**'
(The wisdom of teams by Katzenback & Smith)

WHAT IS A TEAM?

TYPES OF TEAM

'Teams' take many forms and are often referred to as:

- Work teams
- 'Top' teams
- Business strategy teams
- Project teams
- Cross-functional teams
- Task force teams
- Quality circle teams
- Customer service teams
- 'Quick hit' teams
- Maintenance teams
- Sales teams
- Self-managed teams

TEAM POTENTIAL

Teams of people working effectively together can:

- Achieve better results than individuals working alone
- Be more flexible than larger groups
- Take more risks and explore areas that individuals may avoid
- Generate a wider range of ideas than individuals
- Help each other grow in skill and confidence
- Demonstrate commitment not only to the task but to each other
- Motivate themselves

TEAMS VS GROUPS

Despite greater emphasis on teams, very often there is confusion between what exactly is a team and what is a group. Furthermore, the word 'team' is bandied about and applied in situations where the need for a team may not exist.

- Whilst groups can achieve success, they may not be as effective as people working as a team
- People believe that groups will, in time, automatically become teams; sadly, this is not so, as you will read later
- Most of our time is spent in groups at work, at home and in our leisure time, as opposed to teams in the true sense of the word

The differences between the two are subtle yet significant.

TEAMS VS GROUPS

In co-operative groups:

- People work together
- Feelings aren't part of work
- Conflict is accommodated
- Trust and openness are measured
- Information is given on a 'needs to know basis'
- Goals/objectives are either personal or unclear

In effective teams:

- People trust each other
- Feelings are expressed openly
- Conflict is worked through
- People support one another
- Information is shared freely
- Objectives are common to all

TEAMBUILDING VS TEAMWORKING

UNDERSTAND THE DIFFERENCES (1)

A financial services company re-organised and set up customer service teams. This involved staff taking on larger jobs, learning new processes and skills, and developing a new set of relationships with each other.

- In the early stages **teambuilding** was a major feature of the training; this involved giving people a sense of direction, getting to know one another, recognising skills and abilities as well as establishing a method of working

- Once this had been achieved, the emphasis shifted to **teamworking** skills, ie: sharing ideas, co-operating, being open and supporting one another

WHAT IS A TEAM?

TEAMBUILDING VS TEAMWORKING

UNDERSTAND THE DIFFERENCES (2)

The sales director of a multinational company asked for help with teambuilding for his staff. Representatives from each sales area met every two months. With individual targets to reach and incentives based on performance, he was concerned that they were not a team.

- These people worked independently of and in competition with each other; what's more they rarely met - **teambuilding** would not have been appropriate
- However, there was a need to demonstrate the skills of **teamworking** when they met - to co-operate, share ideas and support one another

Teambuilding and teamworking are not the same; the former is often asked for when the latter is required.

- Teambuilding is used to create new teams or review the performance of existing ones
- Teamworking encourages and helps teams succeed, but teamworking by itself never makes a team
- Teamworking is a process, not a goal

WHEN DO YOU NEED A TEAM?

- When you are attempting to deal with genuine problems where nobody knows the answer, if indeed an answer exists (if you have a situation to which the answer is relatively simple, you do not need a team)
- When there is uncertainty about the task, then the greater the need to share the problem with others
- When you are experiencing rapid change
- When there is a need for people to work closely together on real tasks

If you do not fulfil these criteria, you don't need a team.

ONLY WHEN NECESSARY

Remember .....
teams are NOT
the answer to every
organisational need
and situation.
What's more,
wrongly applied,
they can be WASTEFUL
of time and energy.

DIFFICULTIES FACING TEAMS

1. NO ROLE MODELS

- **There are poor examples of teams.**

Why is it a problem?

- Because, without role models there is nobody to follow

Often, those at the top will talk about teams, without really understanding what is involved, or being able to promote the conditions for teamworking within the organisation.

1. NO ROLE MODELS

Recognise that:

- Teams at the top of organisations are the most difficult to create
- People at this level often spend their time on long-term issues and challenges, as well as on activities outside the organisation
- Getting to the top often involves single-minded dedication - a behaviour at odds with the skills required for teams
- People may work by themselves, setting up deals and operating within their own network
- Certainly top teams do not always set the best examples of how to work together; so don't be surprised if people say 'do as I say and not as I do!'

What can you do?

- In this culture, teambuilding is not an easy process, but it is possible as long as you recognise what is happening
- A team leader needs to be aware that skilful use of political skills - to get people at the top to open doors, to support initiatives - can bring rewards and progress

2. NO PERFORMANCE MEASUREMENT

- **The organisation does not measure performance**

Why is it a problem?

- To be effective teams need a demanding performance challenge that is meaningful to all those involved
- Teams need to deliver results - otherwise why have them?
- Without such a challenge, where does a team start to get itself organised and how is success measured?

What can you do?

- Frankly, very little
- Potential teams operating in such a culture will more than likely always be a group, as they have nothing to focus their efforts on

3. TOO MANY TEAMS

- **Teams are seen as the answer to every situation**

Why is it a problem?

- Quite simply, because teams are **not** the solution to all situations.
  If, every time a problem or new challenge arises, the answer is 'let's put together a team', the result will be:
  - an expectation that the situation will be sorted out (quickly); yet, often, the solution lies elsewhere and a team is not the way to find it
  - loss of credibility because teams are being used wrongly

What can you do?

- Try to remind people that teams are only needed when you have real problems to tackle, **to which nobody knows the answer** - if there is an answer

4. EMPHASIS ON INDIVIDUALS

- **Organisation recognises individuals and not teams**

Why is it a problem?

- Teams are often set up as a unit of performance and recognised as such, but:
  - the appraisal scheme is geared to individual performance
  - rewards/salary increases are linked to individual contributions

  As a result individuals may fear that their input will not be recognised or acknowledged and may be reluctant to open up and share ideas.
- Furthermore, within matrix organisations, individuals can be responsible to a functional manager but work as part of a team; this causes its own problems

What can you do?

- In the absence of a reward system for teams, a leader can:
  - actively work to see that individuals are recognised, by promoting their contributions to those in charge
  - have an input to individuals' appraisals by ensuring that your views get back to those doing the appraisals

5. CULTURE OF COMPETITION

- **The organisation's culture does not encourage co-operation**

Why is it a problem?

- Teamworking is about encouraging co-operation and harmony; this will be impossible to achieve if your:
  - structure and systems encourage internal competition and (unhelpful) conflict
  - organisation is not built on trust (why should it suddenly appear in a team?)
  - culture is risk averse; in effective teams, people are encouraged to challenge and extend both their thoughts and actions
- If the culture is one where taking risks is not promoted (and making mistakes is remembered) people will play safe

What can you do?

- Very little
- Individuals by themselves can rarely change the culture

6. TOO MANY PEOPLE

- **The team is too big**

Why is it a problem?

- Because 'teams' of 15-20 people are too big to manage
- The larger they are: the more difficult they are to communicate with and control; the greater the danger that sub-groups will form, increasing the potential for conflict

What can you do?

Bear in mind how size can affect a team's performance and as a leader try to influence the numbers of people you have

TEAM SIZE (GUIDE)

	Under 5	**6-12**	**13-15**	**15+**
Problem solving	3	2	1	4
Speed of judgements	1	2	3	4
Participation by members	1	2	3	4
Cohesion/friendship	1	2	3	4
Consensus	3	2	1	4
Flexibility	1	2	3	4
Individual productivity	2	1	3	4
Group productivity	3	2	1	4

(1 = effective 4 = least effective)

HOW TO BUILD A TEAM

USE PAST EXPERIENCE

Think back on those teams that you may have been part of:

- What were you asked to do?
- How did you go about it?
- Where were you successful and why?
- What difficulties did you come up against?
- How were these overcome?
- How was your team led?
  - What did the leader do well?
  - Where were they not so good?
  - If you were in charge, would you have done anything different?

Look at teams that work within your own organisation and outside (don't forget sporting examples). What lessons can you learn and apply in your own situation?

Caution: if you have been part of a successful team, it is highly unlikely that you can replicate identical conditions in your new team.

CONSULT THE EXPERTS

Much has been written about successful teams. The key points are:

- They need to have something worthwhile to aim for
- They know what they have to achieve
- They need time to develop as a unit
- Team members are clear about their roles
- Team members support each other
- They have worked out a suitable way of working
- They review how they are doing
- They have fun

Above all, successful teams are led, from the front, by people who know what they want, and can inspire others to achieve greatness.

However, in today's business climate:

- Results are expected from newly formed teams faster than ever
- Multidisciplinary teams are common
- Teams contain people from a variety of organisations as well as from different countries and cultures

All of this puts pressure, and a premium, on the skills of the leader. It does not mean that the basic disciplines outlined earlier should be abandoned - indeed just the opposite.

KNOW WHY YOU'RE THERE

Be clear in your own mind what is required of you. Ask those sponsoring the team:

- What do you want us to do, for what reason and by when?
- What's the 'big picture', ie: where does it fit into what's happening elsewhere, inside or outside the organisation?
- Are objectives specific, clear, challenging and measurable? (If not, keep asking questions until they are; this is essential if you want your team to perform.)
- How will you judge our 'success' - what will it look like? It needs to be spelt out in concrete, recognisable terms.
- What resources (people, time, money, facilities, etc) are you making available to us?
- How realistic is it?
- Is there anything we can't do?
- Finally, is there anything we should know but haven't been told?

KNOW WHY YOU'RE THERE

Objectives are key to galvanising the energies, spirit, enthusiasm and skills of all involved.

Remember, a demanding performance challenge creates a team.

This can be work related, eg:

- Developing new products
- Providing a new or better service to customers
- Organising an event by a specific date

Or community based, eg:

- Raising money for a particular cause
- Helping out people in need
  - at particular times of the year, or
  - when tragedy strikes

INVOLVE OTHERS

Make sure that the team knows what it has to achieve. If you are clear in your own mind about what is required, then this will enable you to:

- Have a reference point, the basis for a common purpose and vision to share with others
- Start planning an effective way of working and consider what information is needed from the beginning
- Have a basis against which to measure both performance and progress

However, you still have to get this across to your people. So, give some thought to your first meeting and how you will do this. **After all, here is your first chance to inspire people and make them want to be part of what is on offer!**

INVOLVE OTHERS

VARY THE METHOD

Bear in mind that we take in information through each of our senses - sight, hearing, touch. Some people have a preference for:

- **Pictures and visual images**
  In which case try using a picture, drawing or cartoon
- **Sounds**
  Explain what you are trying to achieve, encourage discussions and invite questions
- **Feelings**
  Give them something to touch or hold (notes summarising the points you are making)

As the first meeting is often crucial to a team's future success, hold it in a different (off site) venue, where the environment is more appealing and you will not get disturbed.

Tip: publish your vision and make sure that your own team as well as your 'customers' have a copy. Pin it on the wall for all to see.

Remember, that to have a vision or mission is fine up to a point, but this still has to be translated into objectives and steps to follow.

IDENTIFY SKILLS AND EXPERIENCES

In an ideal world, effective teams should have a balanced mix of both skill and experience. In practical terms, however, the challenge for many of today's leaders is to blend the best of what they inherit, often within limited timescales.

It will help the group to form if time is spent at an early stage getting members to talk about:

- The skills they have developed, at work and elsewhere
- Their achievements (this despite most people tending to be naturally modest)
- Their experience of working in teams and what they have learnt
- How they prefer to operate, and what they value in others
- What they think they can contribute to the task
- Their interests and what they regard as a worthwhile challenge
- Any initial concerns they may have

Jumping straight into work methods and action planning will be of little value unless you know what is available in your team.

FROM VISION TO GOALS

The secret is not necessarily to have a series of well-written technically correct goals or objectives.

What is needed are statements that capture the imagination and energy of those involved, whilst helping to achieve the vision.

Give some thought to what these ought to be before you meet with your team. However, aim to get buy-in and accountability, rather than impose your own views.

Don't be afraid if team members challenge suggested goals, as this could stimulate debate.

GIVE PEOPLE ROLES

In teams that work well:

- Individuals are clear about the part they are expected to play
- Roles may overlap but they don't conflict
- The mix of roles and skills is sufficient for the task in hand

It is easy to become over concerned with research into team roles, but most leaders do not get the luxury of hand picking their people.

In practical terms, you need people to be flexible if and when circumstances alter. Identifying people's abilities and preferences at the initial team meeting can be helpful both in allocating roles and in times of change.

FIND THE BEST METHOD

Within the group there is likely to be a great deal of experience of how not to do things. You will, no doubt, recall:

- The meetings that overran their planned time
- The group that never made a decision
- The time it took to get authorisation for even the simplest items

Encourage people to share their experiences, so that as a group you can work out the best way to organise yourselves. Suggestions may include:

- Keeping things simple and not over complicating matters
- Not over planning (things can - and inevitably will - change)
- Breaking down large tasks into manageable sections with their own timescales
- Encouraging flexibility and openness to new ideas and methods
- Constantly looking at what you are doing and how (Are there easier ways?)

Work on the basis that the fewer rules the better, as rules reduce freedom and responsibility.

TEAM MEETINGS

Give particular thought to running your team meetings. Consider:

- The purpose of holding meetings in the first place
- How often you need them
- How often people can come together
- Whether the team leader or team members in turn will chair the meetings

The team will need a system for making decisions. Consider:

- Whether you want a formal procedure or an ad hoc method
- What structure you will use for problem solving and evaluating alternatives
- Where the levels of authority will be; who will have the power to decide
- What level of individual decision-making is unacceptable
- How you will get people to buy into the decision
- How you will judge the success of your meetings

Finally, consider ways you can make team meetings inspiring and stimulating. (For practical advice read 'The Meetings Pocketbook' by Patrick Forsyth.)

REVIEW PROGRESS

It is often difficult to find the time to review progress, when caught up in the day-to-day running of a business. However, if you want to be successful, you need to take time out and examine:

- Progress against the goals and objectives that have been set
- How the team is functioning:
  - Openness to people and ideas ('Ah yes, but ...')
  - Co-operation; is it happening?
  - Meetings; productive or a waste of time?
  - Communication; are there gaps?
  - What have people been grumbling about?
  - Conflict; constructive or harmful?
  - Skills and talents; is the team making best use of them?
  - Are we our own worst enemies?
  - Are the real issues being tackled or avoided?
  - What lessons can be learnt?

When group members have time to reflect, they can see more clearly what is essential both in themselves and in others.

HAVE FUN!

Sometimes work can be all too serious.

Teams operating in even the most difficult circumstances still manage to have fun. You can tell this from:

- The 'buzz' and energy about the place
- The smiles on people's faces; they actually look as if they are enjoying their work (How often do you see that?)
- The way they celebrate success

What can **you do** to make work more enjoyable and exciting, and people more enthusiastic?

LEADING THE TEAM

WHAT IS LEADERSHIP?

Leadership is the skill of influencing people towards the achievement of goals or objectives.

Successful leaders have been quoted as:

'Walking a tightrope between the discipline of binding people together and a human touch' (enlisting their hearts)

'Being at their best when people barely know that they exist'

'Demonstrating wisdom by settling for good work and then letting others have the floor'

'Giving staff confidence and the tools to do the job'

'Motivating people to their highest levels by offering them opportunities'

'Using up a great deal of physical and emotional energy'

'Not inflicting pain ... but bearing it'

THE MISSING LEADER

It is generally agreed that teams won't work without leadership, but where are the role models to follow? The quality of leadership affects the whole organisation, yet in many organisations it often seems to be missing altogether.

Frequently, those in leadership positions:

- Have no idea how to get the best from others
- Use fear to get the group going
- Blame others and are not prepared to carry the can
- Seek to grab the credit for good work
- Feel that they should be right all the time
- Spend their time doing and not leading

Only dreadful leaders have bad reputations!

Managing is about:

- Making plans and working out **details**
- Setting up a **structure** so that plans can be met
- **Monitoring** progress against plans
- Producing the **results** that others are expecting

Leading involves:

- Developing a **vision** for the future and where we want to be
- Getting people on board and giving them **direction**
- Motivating, **inspiring** and energising people to overcome any barriers in their way
- Producing **change** in products and methods in order to keep the organisation competitive

LEADERSHIP

Leaders:

- Make things happen
- Inspire, delegate and trust people
- Express their views
- Take risks
- Trouble shoot
- Use tactical planning
- Negotiate and do deals with people
- Trust their judgement
- Accept responsibility
- Achieve results

CAN LEADERSHIP BE LEARNED?

Research indicates that it is not personal characteristics that determine success as a leader, but the way leaders use and blend tasks and relationships to inspire their staff to achieve goals.

- There is **no one common style of leadership and no one best way to lead;** the skill mix required depends upon many variables, the nature of the work and the work group
- **Leaders are not born;** we all have the potential but no gift of leadership (those who do make it inevitably do so by their own efforts and inner drive)
- In truth, **signs of outstanding leadership show most in the quality of others** (the extent to which they are reaching their potential, the way they are learning and whether they regard change as a challenge or not); often these can be people who have little or no job security (e.g. temporary staff and contractors) as well as the high performer

LEADING THE TEAM

HOW TO START

Check your own experience. Ask yourself:

- Have I led work or sporting teams?
  - If so, how successful was I?
  - Where was I strong/vulnerable?
- If your experience is limited:
  - Who has impressed me and can I learn from him/her?
  - What are my natural skills/abilities?
  - How can I use them to the full?

Caution: if you lack confidence in your ability or in the people you have (remember you probably won't be able to hand pick them) then think twice about putting yourself in the position of leader.

Don't worry if you feel that you have not got all the skills. As the task evolves your approach will probably have to change, and you will learn.

Remember, as a leader you need to inspire people. A good start would be to work out what inspires you. How will you communicate that to others?

UNDERSTANDING GROUP BEHAVIOUR

Learn to read what's going on in groups.

You cannot predict how people will behave in groups, no matter how well you know them individually. However, see if you can spot:

The difference between content and process

- When people communicate there are two major ingredients at play:
  - the subject matter on which they are working **(content)**
  - what's happening between the individuals **(process)**
- If we focus only on the **content** we miss picking up the **process**, including the atmosphere created, areas of conflict and emotions between individuals (often a major cause of problems within groups)

How decisions are made

- Keep an eye out to see if the decisions are made:
  - from a logical standpoint or an emotional one
  - by involving everyone or as a result of one person's dominance

UNDERSTANDING GROUP BEHAVIOUR

How people are influenced

- Some people talk a lot but are paid little attention, whereas others may talk less often but are listened to when they do; influence and participation are not the same
- Influence can take many forms; look out for various styles that people use:
  - **autocrat** attempts to impose his/her will on others
  - **peacemaker** tries to prevent conflict or the expression of unpleasant feelings by pouring oil on troubled waters
  - **laissez faire** people seem withdrawn and uninvolved, responding only to others' questions
  - **democrat** works hard to include everyone in the discussion or decision

What the atmosphere is like

- See if you can spot how the group is working and the atmosphere it creates; consider whether it is:
  - friendly or hostile, open or closed
  - and why this should be

UNDERSTANDING GROUP BEHAVIOUR

The rules within the group

- Very often any rules (or norms) are unwritten and, until they have been broken, people don't know that there's a problem!
- Can you spot any behaviours that are acceptable and those that are not?

People who only think of themselves

- See if you can recognise:
  - dominating behaviour (attempted superiority)
  - attacks or blocks on individuals
  - attempts to gain sympathy
  - the person who's fed up and withdrawn
  - joking and ridiculing of others

  This behaviour is not conducive to teamworking.

By being conscious of what is happening, and recognising situations, you can deal with matters before they get out of hand.

DEMONSTRATING LEADERSHIP

The **key** to making teams work is to **demonstrate leadership** and encourage teamworking by:

- Giving people a meaningful and stimulating **challenge**
  - one that will stretch their skills and abilities
- Creating **opportunities** for people to work together
  - look to mix the skills and experiences within the group
- Getting the stronger to **help** the weaker
  - as one way of improving the skills of your people
- **Rotating** jobs and tasks
  - give people the chance of new experiences

DEMONSTRATING LEADERSHIP

The **key** to making teams work is to **demonstrate leadership** and encourage teamworking by:

- **Not** hanging on to positional power; others may have different power bases
  - where this is the case, recognise it and seek to use it for the team's benefit
- Knowing when to **listen**, when to **act** and when to **withdraw**
  - the secret to this is to be in tune with what's happening
- **Explaining** decisions
  - as a way of keeping everyone involved
- Smiling and encouraging **humour**
  - after all, work should be enjoyable

DEMONSTRATING LEADERSHIP

The **key** to making teams work is to **demonstrate leadership** and encourage teamworking by:

- Giving **praise** when it's due
  - say thanks both for good work and when people have made the effort with little to show for it
- **Letting go** and not trying to do everything yourself
  - as a way of demonstrating confidence in others
- Encouraging **open-mindedness;** putting a ban on 'yes, buts!'
  - welcome challenges to how you are currently working
- **Learning** from failures and successes
  - remember, there's no such thing as failure only feedback

DEMONSTRATING LEADERSHIP

The **key** to making teams work is to **demonstrate leadership** and encourage teamworking by:

- Asking for **ideas** and **acting** upon them
  - to show that you are listening to your people
- **Promoting** good ideas (and telling people whose ideas they were)
  - give recognition to others and do not seek to take the glory yourself
- **Simplifying** things: what could we **not** do?
  - cut out time consuming, unproductive ways of working
- Ensuring that people have the **resources** they need to do the job
  - a lot of energy can be wasted if things are not right

DEMONSTRATING LEADERSHIP

The **key** to making teams work is to **demonstrate leadership** and encourage teamworking by:

- Developing **feedback** between team members
  - to identify where more or less must be done
- Running different types of **meetings**
  - change the methods, chairperson, timings, structure, venue
- Giving people a chance to **air their views**
  - have a 'clear the air' or 'How are we doing?' session from time to time
- Encouraging **networking**
  - make and develop contacts outside the group

DEMONSTRATING LEADERSHIP

The **key** to making teams work is to **demonstrate leadership** and encourage teamworking by:

- Promoting a **team identity**
  - to pull the group together
- **Rewarding** the team
  - a difficult area, so ask participants for their ideas
- **Leading** by example
  - do not expect others to do what you would not do
- **Trusting** your people
  - they will not let you down
- **Never assuming**
  - anything!

HANDLING TEAM PROBLEMS

'WE ARE NOT A TEAM'

Teams will not 'happen' overnight as a result of putting people through a series of teambuilding exercises or an outdoor course (whatever your top management believes!). To become a team a group needs to go through certain stages of development.

Kurt Lewis identifies three learning stages:

Freezing - clinging to what is known
Unfreezing - exploring ideas, issues and approaches
Re-freezing - integrating values, attitudes and skills previously held with those needed for the future

According to **Cog's ladder**, groups experience:

Being polite - people try to get to know each other
Asking why we're here - the purpose/aims of the group are established
Bidding for power - people sell their ideas and make a bid for roles
Being constructive - people are willing to change their views
Esprit - high creativity, morale and loyalty are shown

'WE ARE NOT A TEAM'

B W Tuckman cites four stages of team development:

1 Forming

- The group gets together for the first time
- Formal rules/methods of working are yet to be established

2 Storming

- After the relatively polite forming stage, members grow in confidence and an amount of in-fighting is likely

3 Norming

- Now the group moves on to establish norms in the form of systems and procedures, ie: how it should work and a basis for decision making

4 Performing

- Finally, the group becomes far more of a cohesive unit and starts to perform as a team

Some writers refer to 'forming-norming-storming-performing' cycles. My experience is that the storming, or conflict stage, usually precedes the norming or establishing rules phase.

HANDLING TEAM PROBLEMS

'WE ARE NOT A TEAM'

Whilst it is often difficult to identify precisely where a group is, you may well recognise some of the stages and behaviours described.

Helping a group successfully through the various stages, as outlined on the following pages, takes time and effort. How long is difficult to say and almost impossible to predict. It depends on a variety of factors that could include:

- How people in the group get on with each other, which could be influenced by both internal and external events
- Values - the underlying drives influencing the attitude and behaviour of individuals, groups and organisations
- The amount of training and help that the group has received in working through the various stages and any issues raised

Apart from the time involved in creating a team in the true sense, any group can get stuck at any stage of its development. **Progress from one stage to another is not automatic.**

The ability of the leader to recognise what's happening and **take appropriate action** at every stage is crucial to the team's success.

FROM GROUP TO TEAM

STAGE 1: FORMING

Look out for people:

- being polite
- who are guarded in what they say or do (nobody wants to expose themselves)
- who say a lot (often because they are nervous and have not fully understood what's happening), and others who say nothing
- testing each other out

Tips for the leader:

At the first meeting, **be prepared!** It is often how you behave that will dictate the success - or otherwise - of the team. So, give thought to:

- what you want out of it
- who will be coming
- what those coming know about the reasons for setting up the team
- what they will expect
- what experience they can bring
- potential problems/concerns and possible questions
- differences in age and experience, and likely reactions to each other
- how to get them to break the ice and share information, ideas and experiences
- how to put across your vision of what you want the team to achieve

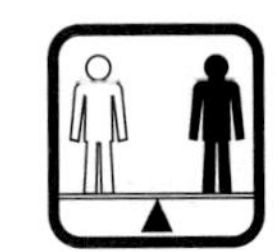

FROM GROUP TO TEAM

STAGE 1: FORMING

Useful ideas:

- If you can select your own team, think about the various areas of skills and knowledge that you need
- If you can't select your team, try making contact with individuals beforehand to talk about the team and what you hope it will achieve; find out what experience they can bring and how they prefer to work
- Look at some of the teambuilding exercises and materials available; of special interest might be icebreakers, sharing skills and experience (as well as contacts) and clarifying objectives/goals
- Draw up a meaningful statement of purpose that the group can:
  - identify with (unlike a broader organisational statement)
  - translate into some form of vision that they can all buy into
- Consider the advantages of holding your first meeting off site

FROM GROUP TO TEAM

STAGE 1: FORMING

Is time on your side?

If you are a new team, then:
- you may have some time before you are expected to deliver results
- people might be patient if you are experiencing teething problems

However:
- if you are providing a service (eg: as do customer or sales support teams) then you may be expected to deliver from day one

Often, lack of time means that you may not be able to work through all the group issues that emerge.

It can be stressful, for both the leader and the team, as they struggle to deliver with all the tensions building up inside the group.

FROM GROUP TO TEAM

STAGE 2: STORMING

Watch out for people:

- expressing opinions about personalities and work methods
- testing the boundaries of roles
- challenging and jockeying for position
- revealing personal agendas
- opting out or feeling trapped
- showing signs of demotivation

For the group to grow, these issues must be worked through, negotiated and resolved in a way that's productive to the individual, group and organisation.

Tips for the leader:

This is a testing time when the group may see you as less dynamic and skilful than at first thought. As a result you could find yourself:

- challenged and threatened by one or more individuals in the group (indeed the group may demand a change of leader owing to a mismatch of skills, values and experience)
- sitting in the middle of a group which has split and is taking sides as to who should lead (this 'us and them' attitude may continue even if a new leader is appointed)

FROM GROUP TO TEAM

STAGE 2: STORMING

Useful ideas:

- Watch what's happening in the business and consider what people may be expecting from your team; team sponsors can get frustrated if results don't appear to be achieved as quickly as expected, in which case they might look for scapegoats
- Ensure what you produce is up to standard and meets requirements; you could have spent a lot of time arguing amongst yourselves about working methods, while ignoring the real needs of the customers
- Watch out for rumours starting to emerge that people aren't happy
- Make sure that you meet deadlines, or you could be called to account for the actions - or inactions - of your team

FROM GROUP TO TEAM

STAGE 2: STORMING

Actions to take:

A difficult stage. One of your best tactics is to anticipate it coming and invite questions/opinions, sooner rather than later.

Be proactive (and provocative) by calling a meeting to look, in particular, at other ways of operating:

- invite people to come prepared to challenge what's been suggested and offer alternatives

Look out for signs of conflict: note the non-verbals, the put-downs and people's reactions to certain group members (see section on group behaviour)

Lead from the front; deal with situations as they arise

FROM GROUP TO TEAM

STAGE 3: NORMING

Be prepared for:

- norms (ie: standards or ground rules) starting to emerge that could influence behaviour through, for example: acceptable/unacceptable behaviour; the language people use; how secret or open they are

This process is often helped by the need and pressures to produce results. The very act of teams having to organise themselves can mean that work issues are confronted and skill levels of team members are identified.

Tips for the leader:

You will, no doubt, be showing signs of relief that a lot of the tensions of stage two are over and that you have got this far! However, you still need to:

- help any new members into the team by explaining what you are doing and why; this could save time later
- keep an open mind and look for new ideas (in fact actively seek to promote them)
- allow group members to get organised; they may simply want you to arrange for resources to be made available
- keep contact and don't allow members to go their own way

FROM GROUP TO TEAM

STAGE 3: NORMING

Useful ideas:

- Recognise that you now have the potential to become a team in the true sense
- To move on to the next stage, the leader has to find ways of helping members identify with each other:
  - listen to and watch what's going on
  - act as a mediator between opposing sides
  - offer to listen to their problems or views
  - try to get group members to identify with an overall mission or purpose (a meaningful identity with which to go forward)

  You might have explained it at the first meeting but, after all the in-fighting that's taken place, it's time for a recap.

Beware:

- At this stage there is often a real danger that the group could slip back into the storming stage; the very act of trying to achieve a task can bring into question the practices, values and ideas established earlier
- Newcomers to the group may challenge what's in place and in so doing re-create earlier tensions

FROM GROUP TO TEAM

STAGE 4: PERFORMING

You will notice:

- Problems get solved and work gets done
- Team members are more supportive of each other
- Information and ideas are shared
- Greater tolerance and flexibility
- More humour, energy and openness
- Nothing is too much trouble; no challenge too difficult

FROM GROUP TO TEAM

STAGE 4: PERFORMING

Tips for the leader:

Don't allow yourself the luxury of sitting back and relaxing after a job well done: the team could carry on performing well for a long time to come, or it could **slip back into any of the earlier stages.**

This will depend upon:

- how many people leave the team and how well newcomers are integrated (successful teams can often make it difficult for newcomers to join; such is the closeness of the unit that any new person or ideas are sometimes rejected - see section on 'Groupthink')
- how far the business climate remains the same; a shift in direction could force the team to reassess all areas including skills-base

At the performing stage there is much that the leader can do to encourage teamwork (see the leadership section for ideas).

CONFLICT

Conflict can often be good for a group. It may bring out new ideas and raise new issues. Conflict is natural; the skill is to turn this into a creative force.

Whilst one of the strengths of a team is the variety of members' opinions and experiences, sometimes this can get out of hand. Comments become personal, individuals are picked upon by other members of the group, and time is spent settling old scores and not getting on with the task at hand.

This can lead to **unhealthy** conflict, one of the biggest barriers to team performance. Should this be the case, positive action has to be taken.

CONFLICT

It is usually down to the team leader to deal with any (destructive) conflicts that may arise. These are common at the storming stage, where skilful handling is vital if progress is to be made.

The skill is to stand back and take a good look (a so-called 'helicopter view') at the behaviour that's taking place **before acting**.

There are many ways of handling conflict:

ASSERTIVENESS	UNCO-OPERATIVE		CO-OPERATIVE
ASSERTIVE	**COMPETING (WIN-LOSE)**		**COLLABORATING (WIN-WIN)**
		COMPROMISING (WIN-WIN)	
UNASSERTIVE	**AVOIDING (LOSE-LOSE)**		**ACCOMMODATING (LOSE-WIN)**

CO-OPERATIVENESS

Based on the Thomas - Kilmann Conflict Mode Instrument.

CONFLICT

Competing (win-lose) - handling conflict head on by standing firm and rejecting the ideas of others

Collaborating (win-win) - taking the ideas of both parties and finding ways of developing them all

Compromising (win-win) - the art of win-win negotiations

Avoiding (lose-lose) - not getting involved in the conflict

Accommodating (lose-win) - accepting the situation and agreeing to back down

Whatever style is used it is important that conflict is not ignored. Look to resolve it in whatever way is appropriate. Remember, team members do not have to like one another.

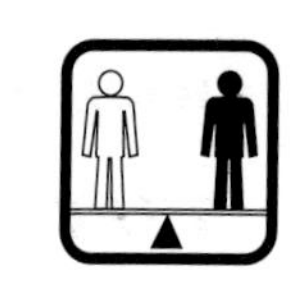

CONFLICT

BE ASSERTIVE

- Join the other person(s) in working towards a win/win outcome
- Keep a clear picture of the person and yourself separate from the issue
- Make clear 'I' statements
- Be clear about your perception of the conflict and your preferred outcome
- Take one issue at a time
- Look and listen to each other
- Ensure that you understand each other
- Open your minds to creative ways of sorting out the conflict
- Choose a mutually convenient time and place for discussion
- Acknowledge and appreciate each other
- Recognise that silence is a great source of strength

LEADERSHIP STYLE

Great leaders tend to lead from the front and their style can have a dramatic impact on the performance of their teams.

Styles range from:

Controller	Who wants plans carried out:	- issues specific instructions - supervises closely
Guide	Who clarifies the task:	- offers advice - gets members to feel ownership of the task
Consultant	Who broadly outlines the task:	- invites discussion and ideas - ensures team agrees action
Facilitator	Who gives overall direction:	- delegates full responsibility to the team - expects team to report on progress

Leaders become impressive when they **stop** trying to impress. When they attempt to make themselves look good, the group knows and dislikes this.

LEADERSHIP STYLE

If you are a leader, the style you adopt and its effectiveness often depend upon the nature of your followers as well as the organisation in which you work.

Think about the sort of followers you have (there are more followers than leaders):

- Are they the type of people who follow unwillingly, and treat everything you say with caution or, as is increasingly the case, do they expect to be involved in what's happening?
- How well do they work together? How mature is the leader/follower relationship? And at what stage of its development is the group?

Perhaps the biggest mistake anyone can make is to adopt one style to all, changing, situations and circumstances.

Once again, keep an eye on what's happening in the group. Don't be afraid to ask for feedback on how you are coming across; be prepared to change if necessary to match the situation. Remember, you are dealing with human beings and not numbers.

HANDLING TEAM PROBLEMS

LACK OF BALANCE

Imagine working with a group of people who all wanted to be in charge or who were so cautious that nothing ever happened. Without the mix of skills needed to create a balanced team you would not get very far.

In successful teams you need someone to:

- **Be creative** and come up with imaginative ideas.
  Without ideas - even if they are sometimes 'off the wall' - how else will teams make progress?
- **Take the chair**, pull people together and give structure to the group.
  They do not have to be the chosen leader, but without their skills the group could go round in circles and make little forward progress.

LACK OF BALANCE

In successful teams you need someone to:

- **Give direction** by pulling ideas together and looking for practical ways of pushing the group into making decisions. Often such people are the appointed leaders and they are needed because sooner or later the talking will have to stop and action must start.
- **Promote unity** amongst the group by being aware of how people are feeling, pick up the vibes of what's happening and show loyalty to colleagues. Without such a person it is easy for the group to become divided, especially when under pressure.
- **Worry about schedules, deadlines and what might go wrong**. Although these people might cause frustration with their obsession for detail, they do at least ensure that nothing is overlooked and jobs are delivered on time.

LACK OF BALANCE

In successful teams you need someone to:

- **Organise people** by converting decisions and plans into practical tasks that others can get on with. Without this there is a danger that little or nothing will happen.
- **Find out what's needed** by using a range of contacts, often outside the group. These people are the 'fix-its' of the team, the source of much information and many ideas. Their value is to prevent the team losing touch with reality and safeguarding delivery, especially when the pressure is on.
- **Analyse situations** and information from a variety of sources. The great strength of such people is to stop the group committing themselves to a wrong course of action.

KEEPING A BALANCE

- A well-balanced team has people who can cover each role/part. This is not to say that you always need eight people in a team: whilst everyone has a preferred team role, most people are capable of playing a secondary role should the need arise.
- Successful teams are not obsessed by matching people to role categories; however, they acknowledge that:
  - members may have to take on more than one role (especially in small teams);
  - not all roles may be essential, as with a project divided into phases which has members joining as it progresses;
  - skilled leaders make the best of their resources, especially with inherited - rather than selected - teams.
- In practical terms, look at what your team needs and the skills that you have available; could it be that roles emerge for people?

SKILLS SHORTAGE

If the team is failing to perform, perhaps its members lack basic skills. Or, the mix and breadth of skills are not sufficient for the task in hand.

A properly functioning team will allow its members to learn new skills; there is no need to import new people. However, you may be some way off being a team, so:

- Try and **identify the skills needed** before you select or inherit the group.
- **Build up a skills inventory** of the people you have (there are tests around to identify the various skills/attributes). How far does it match what you require? How can you bridge the gap? (There are many ways to develop people other than sending them on courses; see 'The Manager's Training Pocketbook' for stimulating ideas).

REMINDER: Don't forget, most people have a lot of skills and abilities. They are just waiting for the chance to use them.

PERFORMANCE ISSUES IGNORED

There is a real chance that the team will not achieve its goals if performance is not up to standard or is an issue. This can happen, for example, when:

- Poor performance is tolerated
- Good performance is not recognised
- The push for team effort disguises individual weaknesses/talent
- Team output is poor mainly because individual team members are weak

Tips:

- At the start make sure that the team is clear about when it has to achieve (its objectives) and how well it has to perform (the acceptable standards)
- Offer help in the form of training and support where necessary
- Introduce a way of checking performance and make it an item at team meetings
- Examine the causes of any performance problems before rushing in with an instant solution
- Encourage self-appraisal of skills as well as feedback between members

For a team to be successful, performance - or lack of it - has to be addressed head on by the leader. Remember, the team is only as good as its weakest member.

LACK OF DISCIPLINE

A team needs to have rules and a certain amount of discipline in order to give itself structure. However, very often:

- The organisation keeps changing those rules, pulling individuals out and substituting new people
- The team values getting on well above working well
- There's a lot of self-orientated behaviour; individuals look to promote themselves at the expense of others in the team

If this occurs:

- Ask yourself, 'Is what's happening within my control?'

  (Typically, if the organisation makes changes there is little you can do bar making people aware of the implications. Often, you will have to start your teambuilding efforts again and re-negotiate timescales - if you're lucky. More often than not, you could still be expected to meet your original commitments!)
- If it's happening within the team, quickly make people aware of its effects and what it is doing to the team.

SHORT ON IDEAS

Creativity and innovation are essential for any team. New ideas and solutions are needed to tackle many of today's problems; what worked yesterday may just about work today but almost certainly will not work tomorrow.

You can recognise if your team has stopped being creative when they:
- fail to challenge, even the obvious
- restrict their thinking to (self) imposed boundaries
- give the answer that they think is expected as opposed to what might be possible
- keep 'yes, butting' every suggestion and the team's 'ideas' person becomes frustrated

What can you do?

- Look at areas where new ideas are needed, eg: improvements to product or service, methods of working, more effective use of skills and resources
- Bear in mind that creativity, a thinking process that helps generate new ideas, can be developed; there are many ways other than brainstorming ('The Creative Manager's Pocketbook' will show you how)
- Pick up on examples where people are closing their minds to new ideas
- Hold idea-generating sessions; for every 'yes, but', challenge it with a 'what if?' statement

NO ENTHUSIASM FOR TEAMS

What can you do?

You can't force people to become a team. At best, all you can do is try to persuade them of the benefits that could be gained if they worked together and shared their skills and expertise with others. If people are still anti the thought, try adopting a low-key approach:

- Get them to work with one or two people on a particular task
- Call a team meeting but **don't** invite them; instead, have a word and explain that you know that they don't want to be part of a team so you haven't involved them (you may be surprised at their reaction)

SUCCESSFUL TEAMS

RECOGNITION

Successful teams can be recognised by:

- Their **commitment** towards each other and to achieving goals
- The **climate** they create in which people feel comfortable and able to take risks
- The **openness and honesty** developed as people try to resolve situations and not create barriers
- How they constantly look to **improve** what they do and how they tackle situations
- Their ability to **analyse and solve problems**, and their commitment to the solution
- How they **use resources** within the team to the best effect
- Their active **encouragement** of different opinions and ideas
- The **results** they achieve

HOW TO LEAD

The best way is often not to lead! At this stage of the group's development, the style needs to be more 'hands off', as opposed to 'hands on'.

What's more, in successful groups, shared leadership is a common feature, especially when particular knowledge or experience is required.

So, as leader, don't feel that you have to hang on to your power and status. Having said this, teams will still require the leader to maintain direction, guidance, energy and commitment.

A key role will be to look for support and resources from within the organisation.

Frequently, teams will seek protection from the outside, so that they can get on with the job in hand. However, beware: here lies a potential recipe for disaster and eventual downfall, should the team become too introspective.

DANGERS

Successful teams can run into danger if they:

- Get a good reputation and rest on their laurels
- Believe that they are invincible and can do no wrong
- Close ranks and make it difficult for newcomers to get in
- Spend so long looking inwards that they fail to see what's happening to the outside world
- Become complacent and suffer from 'Groupthink'

'Groupthink' occurs when:

- The culture of the group becomes so strong that members think only of themselves and ignore the task
- Group influences moderate extreme views such that there is a move towards a risk-avoiding compromise
- Concern for solidarity outweighs the ability to think sensibly

MORE ABOUT 'GROUPTHINK'

'Groupthink' can also occur when:

- Reality is distorted and crucial information is ignored
- Reasons for maintaining group feelings are found, rather than rethinking a problem
- Discussion of threatening possibilities is avoided
- Those who oppose the group are classed as evil, weak or stupid
- Silence is interpreted as consent

'Groupthink' can lead to the group:

- Failing to solve its problems effectively
- Discussing only a minimum number of alternatives
- Following courses of action, favoured by the majority of the group, without examining hidden risks or alternatives
- Failing to use expertise available to the group

Studies of American foreign policy 'disasters', including the Bay of Pigs, Korea and Vietnam, attributed failure to 'Groupthink'. For more information, read Irving Janis' 'Victims of Group Think'.

SUCCESSFUL TEAMS

A FINAL THOUGHT

Sport provides rich examples of successful teams:

- From the professionals who have honed their skills and disciplines to perfection and seen off all the opposition, to the . . .
- Underdogs who have succeeded against all the odds on a particular day

Sport also shows us that:

- Even the most successful teams can just as easily lose their edge if they:
  - hang on to players who are past their best
  - fail to adapt to changing situations
  - do not introduce new talent and tactics
  - ignore what the opposition is doing
- Simply selecting the best players won't guarantee a winning team

Considerable time, effort, skill and hard work go into making teams successful: 10% inspiration, 90% perspiration! Getting there is relatively easy - **staying there** is more difficult.

So, good luck.

READING LIST/REFERENCES

'The Wisdom of Teams' by Jon Katzenbach and Douglas Smith,
Harvard Business School Press.
A stimulating and well written account of teamworking from a pragmatic viewpoint. The book makes a clear distinction between working groups and teams, and challenges many conventional ideas.

'Leading your Team' by Andrew Leigh and Michael Maynard,
Nicholas Brealey Publishing.
An excellent practical account of how to involve and inspire teams in today's business climate. Contains lots of ideas on setting up and running teams.

'Leadership is an Art' by Max De Pree, Arrow Business Books.
Read one man's vision of leadership - it will only take you an hour - and enjoy its refreshingly simple approach.

'The Tao of Leadership' by John Heider, Gower.
Wisdom passed down over the centuries from one of China's best loved books. Learn how to unite the skills of leading with your way of life.

About the Author

Ian Fleming, MA DMS Dip Ed, works as a freelance management trainer. With a preference for coaching rather than lecturing, his approach is to work mainly in-company helping managers and teams tackle real issues.

This is his fourth title in the Pocketbook Series and is based on his practical experience of helping groups who are stuck on the journey of trying to become a team.

Should you wish to talk to Ian about his ideas and approach, contact him at:
2 Robins Orchard, Chalfont St Peter, Bucks, SL9 0HQ.
(Tel: 01494 873623)

Acknowledgement: To the many teams I have worked with over the years, and colleagues for their input. Written in memory of Pat - together we were a team.

First published in 1996 by Management Pocketbooks Limited,
14 East Street, Alresford, Hampshire SO24 9EE

Printed in England by Alresford Press Limited, Alresford, Hampshire SO24 9QF

 ISBN 1 870471 36 9

The Management Pocketbook Series

- The Appraisals Pocketbook
- The Balance Sheet Pocketbook
- The Business Presenter's Pocketbook
- The Business Writing Pocketbook
- Challengers!
- The Communicator's Pocketbook
- The Creative Manager's Pocketbook
- The Cultural Gaffes Pocketbook
- The Customer Service Pocketbook
- The Export Pocketbook
- The Interviewer's Pocketbook
- The Key Accounts Manager's Pocketbook
- The Learner's Pocketbook
- The Managing Budgets Pocketbook
- The Managing Cashflow Pocketbook
- The Managing Change Pocketbook
- The Managing Your Appraisal Pocketbook
- The Manager's Pocketbook
- The Manager's Training Pocketbook
- The Marketing Pocketbook
- The Meetings Pocketbook
- The Negotiator's Pocketbook
- The People Manager's Pocketbook
- The Quality Pocketbook
- The Salesperson's Pocketbook
- The Team Builder's Pocketfile of Ready-to-copy Exercises
- The Teamworking Pocketbook
- The Telesales Pocketbook
- The Time Management Pocketbook
- Tips for Presenters audio cassette
- Tips for Trainers audio cassette
- The Trainer Standards Pocketbook
- The Trainer's Pocketbook
- The Trainer's Pocketbook of Ready-to-use Exercises

ORDER FORM

Please send me .... copies of 'The Teamworking Pocketbook'

.... copies of ....Pocketbook

.... copies of ....Pocketbook

.... copies of ....Pocketbook

.... copies of ....Pocketbook

Name .... Position ....

Company ....

Address ....

....

....

....

Telephone .... Fax ....

VAT No. (EC companies) ..... Your Order Ref ....

Management Pocketbooks Ltd
14 East Street, Alresford
Hampshire SO24 9EE
Tel: (01962) 735573
Fax: (01962) 733637